Simple

Indian Cuisine

Cookbook with 80 Easy-to-Follow and Delicious Comfort Food Recipes and Regional Specialties

Lakshmi Thakur

Introduction

Welcome to "Simple Authentic Indian Cuisine," a culinary voyage into the heart of India's culinary heritage.

As you unfold the pages of this book, you're not just stepping into a collection of recipes, but an intimate exploration of the Indian kitchen's soul. Each recipe you encounter here is a testament to India's food philosophy - the delicate interplay of spices, the joy of simple ingredients coming together, and the universal comfort found in a home-cooked meal.

Indian food is an intricate dance of flavors and textures, a medley of regional influences and individual interpretations. In the hands of a loving cook, humble ingredients evolve into a warm bowl of dal, fragrant biryani, or delectable paneer curry. The spices, as varied as India's landscapes, aren't merely about adding heat but offering a complexity and depth that makes each dish unique and satisfying.
In this collection, I guide you gently through the vast expanse of Indian cuisine, simplifying techniques, and sharing secrets I have gathered over years. Each recipe, each technique, is a distillation of tradition, personal experience, and the joy of creation.

This book is more than a cookbook. It is a tribute to the Indian culinary tradition, a nod to every grandmother, mother, and aunt who have poured love into their cooking, making meals that touch not just our taste buds but also our hearts.
As you delve into this book, I hope it fills your kitchen with inviting aromas, your plates with beautiful, nourishing meals, and your life with the timeless pleasure of delightful food.
So, dear reader, together let us embark on this flavorful journey, exploring the authentic, comforting, and delectable world of Indian cuisine, one recipe at a time.

Happy cooking!
Lakshmi Thakur

Contents

APPETIZERS & STARTERS

Masala Dosa

PREP: *8 hour* **COOK:** *30 Mins* **Servings:** *4*

1 cup long-grain rice (200 g)
¼ cup urad dal (split black lentils) (50 grams)
½ teaspoon fenugreek seeds
Salt to taste
Water for soaking and grinding
4 medium-sized potatoes, boiled and mashed
1 tablespoon vegetable oil
1 teaspoon mustard seeds
1 teaspoon cumin seeds
1 medium-sized onion, chopped
2-3 green chilies, finely chopped
½-inch ginger, grated
8-10 curry leaves
1/4 teaspoon turmeric powder
Salt to taste
Water as needed
2 tablespoons fresh cilantro (coriander) leaves, chopped

1. Soak rice, urad dal, and fenugreek seeds separately for 4-5 hours.
2. Drain and grind together with water to make a smooth batter. Add salt and ferment for 6-7 hours or overnight.
3. Heat oil in a pan. Add mustard seeds, cumin seeds, onions, green chilies, ginger, and curry leaves. Sauté until onions turn translucent.
4. Add turmeric powder, mashed potatoes, salt, and water. Cook for 2-3 minutes. Garnish with coriander leaves.
5. Heat a non-stick or cast-iron skillet. Pour dosa batter, spread it in a circular motion, and cook until golden brown on both sides.
6. Serve hot with coconut chutney and sambar.

Aloo Paratha

PREP: *20 Mins* **COOK:** *20 Mins* **Servings:** *4*

Dough:
2 cups whole wheat flour (260g)
1/2 teaspoon salt
Water as needed

Potato Filling:
4 medium-sized potatoes, boiled and mashed
1 small onion, finely chopped
2 green chilies, finely chopped
1/2 teaspoon cumin seeds
1/2 teaspoon red chili powder
1/2 teaspoon garam masala
Salt to taste
Fresh cilantro (coriander) leaves, finely chopped
Vegetable oil for cooking

1. In a bowl, toss the whole wheat flour and salt. Gradually add water (add in portions, not all at once) and knead into a soft dough. Cover and set aside.
2. Mix mashed potatoes, chopped onion, green chilies, cumin seeds, red chili powder, garam masala, salt, and coriander leaves in another bowl. Mix well. Divide the dough into equal-sized balls and flatten each ball with your hands.
3. Place a portion of the potato filling in the center of each flattened dough ball. Bring the edges to each other and seal the filling inside the dough.
4. Roll out each filled dough ball into a round paratha, dusting it with flour as needed.
5. Heat a tawa/griddle or large pan over medium heat. Place the rolled paratha/flattened dough on the tawa and cook until golden brown, applying oil as needed.
6. Remove from the tawa and repeat the process with the remaining dough and filling.
7. Serve hot with yogurt, pickle, or chutney.

Idli with Sambar

PREP: *8 hour* **COOK:** *30 Mins* **Servings:** *4*

Idli Batter:
2 cups idli rice (400g)
½ cup urad dal (split black lentils) (105g)
½ teaspoon fenugreek seeds
Salt to taste
Water for soaking and grinding

Sambar:
½ cup toor dal (split pigeon peas)
1 small onion, chopped
1 small tomato, chopped
1 small carrot, chopped
1 small potato, chopped
¼ cup tamarind pulp (40g)
1 tablespoon sambar powder
¼ teaspoon turmeric powder
Salt to taste
1 tablespoon vegetable oil
1/2 teaspoon mustard seeds
8-10 curry leaves

1. Soak idli rice with urad dal and fenugreek seeds separately in water for 4-5 hours.
2. Drain and grind the soaked rice, urad dal, and fenugreek seeds with water to make a smooth batter. Add salt and let it ferment for 6-7 hours or overnight.
3. Grease the idli molds and pour the batter into each mold. Steam the idlis in a steamer for 10-12 minutes or until cooked.
4. In a separate pot, cook toor dal with water, chopped onion, tomato, carrot, potato, tamarind pulp, sambar powder, turmeric powder, and salt until the dal is cooked.
5. Heat oil in a pan. Add mustard seeds and curry leaves. Let them splutter. Pour the tempering over the cooked dal mixture and mix well. Serve hot with coconut chutney.

Upma

PREP: *10 Mins* **COOK:** *20 Mins* **Servings:** *4*

1 cup (200 grams) semolina (rava or sooji)
2 tablespoons vegetable oil
1 teaspoon mustard seeds
1 teaspoon cumin seeds
1 medium onion, finely chopped
2 green chilies, finely chopped
½-inch ginger, grated
8-10 curry leaves
1 medium carrot, finely chopped
¼ cup (40 grams) green peas
2 cups water (480g)
Salt to taste
Fresh cilantro (coriander) leaves, chopped (for garnish)
Lemon wedges (optional)

1. Dry roast the semolina over medium heat until it turns golden brown. Remove from heat and set aside.
2. Heat oil in a pan. Add mustard seeds and cumin seeds. Let them splutter.
3. Add chopped onions, green chilies, ginger, and curry leaves. Sauté until onions turn translucent.
4. Add chopped carrot and green peas. Cook for a few minutes until the vegetables are tender.
5. Add water and salt. Bring it to a boil.
6. Gradually add the roasted semolina, stirring continuously to avoid lumps.
7. Reduce the heat, keep cover, and cook for about 5-7 minutes until the semolina absorbs the water and becomes fluffy.
8. Garnish with fresh coriander leaves. Serve hot with lemon wedges (if desired).

Poha

PREP: *10 Mins* **COOK:** *15 Mins* **Servings:** *4*

- 2 cups flattened rice (poha) (300g)
- 2 tablespoons vegetable oil
- 1 teaspoon mustard seeds
- 1 teaspoon cumin seeds
- 1 medium onion, finely chopped
- 2 green chilies, slit
- 8-10 curry leaves
- 1/2 teaspoon turmeric powder
- Salt to taste
- Fresh cilantro (coriander) leaves, chopped (for garnish)
- Lemon wedges (for serving)

1. Rinse the flattened rice (poha) in water a couple of times. Drain and set aside.
2. Heat oil in a pan. Add mustard seeds and cumin seeds. Let them splutter.
3. Add chopped onions with green chilies and curry leaves. Sauté until onions turn translucent.
4. Add turmeric powder and mix well.
5. Add the rinsed flattened rice (poha) and salt. Mix gently until well combined. Cook for 3-4 minutes until heated through.
6. Garnish with fresh coriander leaves.
7. Serve hot with lemon wedges.

Rava Dosa

PREP: *10 Mins* **COOK:** *20 Mins* **Servings:** *4*

1 cup semolina (rava or sooji) (180g)
½ cup rice flour (155g)
¼ cup all-purpose flour (maida) (30g)
2 tablespoons fine semolina (optional)
1 teaspoon cumin seeds
1/2 teaspoon black pepper powder
Salt to taste
2 cups water (480g)
Vegetable oil for cooking

1. Combine semolina, rice flour, all-purpose flour, fine semolina, cumin seeds, black pepper powder, and salt in a mixing bowl.
2. Gradually add water and whisk to make a thin, lump-free batter. Let it rest for 10 minutes.
3. Put the cast-iron skillet over medium heat. Grease it lightly with oil.
4. Drop a ladleful of batter onto the center of the skillet and spread it in a circular motion to form a thin dosa.
5. Drizzle a little oil around the edges of the dosa. Cook until the edges turn crispy and golden brown.
6. Flip the dosa and cook the other side for a minute. Remove the dosa from the skillet and keep it aside.
7. Repeat the process with the leftover batter to make more dosas. Serve hot with coconut chutney or sambar.

Medu Vada

PREP: *15 Mins* **COOK:** *20 Mins* **Servings:** *4*

1 cup urad dal (split black lentils) (210g)
1 tablespoon rice flour
1 teaspoon cumin seeds
1 small onion, finely chopped
2 green chilies, finely chopped
8-10 curry leaves, chopped
½-inch ginger, grated
Salt to taste
Vegetable oil for deep frying

1. First, Wash, then soak the urad dal in water for 4-5 hours. Drain well.
2. Grind the soaked urad dal (just urad dal, not water) to a smooth batter, adding very little water if needed.
3. Transfer the batter to a mixing bowl. Add rice flour, cumin seeds, chopped onions, green chilies, curry leaves, ginger, and salt. Mix well.
4. Heat vegetable oil in a deep-frying pan or kadai over medium heat.
5. Wet your hands with water. Shape a small portion of the batter into a round vada. Make a hole in the center using your thumb.
6. Gently slide the shaped vada into the hot oil and deep fry until crispy on both sides.
7. Remove the vadas and drain on a paper towel to remove excess oil. Serve hot.

Paneer Bhurji

PREP: *10 Mins* **COOK:** *15 Mins* **Servings:** *4*

7 oz (200 grams) paneer (Indian cottage cheese), crumbled
2 tablespoons vegetable oil
1 teaspoon cumin seeds
1 medium onion, finely chopped
1 medium tomato, finely chopped
2 green chilies, finely chopped
1/2 teaspoon turmeric powder
1/2 teaspoon red chili powder
Salt to taste
Fresh cilantro (coriander) leaves, chopped (for garnish)

1. Heat oil in a pan. Add cumin seeds and let them splutter.
2. Add chopped onions and sauté until they turn translucent.
3. Add chopped tomatoes and green chilies. Cook until tomatoes are soft and mushy.
4. Add turmeric, red chili powder, and salt. Mix well.
5. Add crumbled paneer and mix gently to combine with the spices. Cook for a few minutes until heated through.
6. Garnish with fresh coriander leaves.
7. Serve hot with roti, naan, or rice.

Besan Chilla

PREP: *10 Mins* **COOK:** *15 Mins* **Servings:** *4*

1 cup besan (gram flour) (90g)
¼ cup finely chopped onions (50g)
¼ cup finely chopped tomatoes
2 green chilies, finely chopped
1/2 teaspoon turmeric powder
1/2 teaspoon red chili powder
Salt to taste
Water as needed
Vegetable oil for cooking

1. Combine besan, chopped onions, tomatoes, green chilies, turmeric, red chili powder, and salt.
2. Gradually add water and whisk to make a smooth batter. The batter should have a pouring consistency.
3. Put the cast-iron skillet over medium heat. Grease it lightly with oil.
4. Drop a ladleful of batter onto the center of the skillet and spread it in a circular motion to form a thin pancake.
5. Drizzle a little oil around the edges of the chilla. Cook until the edges turn crispy and golden brown.
6. Flip and cook the other side for a minute. Remove the chilla from the skillet and keep it aside.
7. Repeat the process with the leftover batter to make more chillas.
8. Serve hot with ketchup or mint chutney.

Gobi Paratha

PREP: *20 Mins* **COOK:** *30 Mins* **Servings:** *4*

Dough:
2 cups whole wheat flour (260g)
Water as needed
Salt to taste

Gobi Stuffing:
2 cups (200g) grated cauliflower (gobi)
1 small onion, finely chopped
1 green chili, finely chopped
1/2 teaspoon grated ginger
1/2 teaspoon cumin seeds
1/2 teaspoon turmeric powder
1/2 teaspoon red chili powder
Salt to taste
Fresh cilantro (coriander) leaves, chopped
Ghee or vegetable oil for cooking

1. In a bowl, toss the whole wheat flour and salt.Add water in portions and knead into a soft dough. Cover and set aside. Heat ghee/oil in a pan. Add cumin seeds and let them splutter. Add chopped onions, green chili, and grated ginger. Sauté until onions turn translucent.
2. Add grated cauliflower and cook for a few minutes.Add turmeric, red chili powder, and salt. Mix well to coat the cauliflower. Cook for a few more minutes. Remove from heat and cool, then divide the dough into equal-sized balls.
3. Take one and roll it into a small circle. Place a portion of the cauliflower stuffing in the center. Bring the edges together and seal. Flatten the dough ball to flatten it out gently. Heat a tawa/griddle over medium heat. Add ghee/oil to cook the paratha. Remove this and repeat the process with the leftover.

Rava Idli

PREP: *15 MIns* **COOK:** *20 Mins* **Servings:** *4*

- 1 cup semolina (180g) (rava or sooji)
- 1 cup yogurt (240g) (or dairy-free alternative)
- ¼ cup (35g) finely chopped carrots
- ¼ cup (35g) finely chopped green peas
- 2 tablespoons finely chopped cilantro (coriander) leaves
- 1 tablespoon grated coconut (optional)
- 1/2 teaspoon baking soda
- Salt to taste
- Water as needed
- Vegetable oil for greasing

1. Combine semolina, yogurt, chopped carrots, chopped green peas, coriander leaves, grated coconut (if using), baking soda, and salt in a mixing bowl. Mix well.
2. Add water gradually to form a thick yet pourable batter. Let the batter rest for 10 minutes.
3. Grease the idli molds with oil.
4. Fill the idli molds with the batter. Steam the idlis in a steamer for 15-20 minutes or until cooked.
5. Remove the idlis from the molds and let them cool slightly before serving.
6. Serve hot with coconut chutney and sambar.

Uttapam

PREP: *10 Mins* **COOK:** *15 Mins* **Servings:** *4*

Dosa Batter:
1 cup rice (200g)
¼ cup urad dal (55g) (split black lentils)
½ teaspoon fenugreek seeds
Salt to taste
Water for soaking and grinding

Uttapam:
2 cups dosa batter
1 small onion, finely chopped
1 small tomato, finely chopped
1 small green bell pepper, finely chopped
2 tablespoons finely chopped cilantro (coriander) leaves
2-3 green chilies, finely chopped
Salt to taste
Vegetable oil for cooking

1. Rinse and soak rice, urad dal, and fenugreek seeds for 4-5 hours. Drain and grind with water into a thick, pourable batter.
2. Mix in salt and let ferment overnight. Heat a skillet, take two cups batter, and spread onto skillet.
3. Top with chopped vegetables and salt, drizzle oil around edges and top. Cook until both sides are golden.
4. Repeat with remaining batter and serve hot.

SNACKS AND STREET FOOD

Samosa

PREP: *30 Mins* **COOK:** *20 Mins* **Servings:** *8*

Dough:

2 cups all-purpose flour (240g)
1/2 teaspoon salt
4 tablespoons vegetable oil
Water as needed

Filling:

2 medium potatoes, boiled and mashed (200 grams)
1/2 cup green peas (80 grams)
1 small onion, finely chopped (100 grams)
2 green chilies, finely chopped
1 teaspoon ginger-garlic paste
1 teaspoon cumin seeds
1 teaspoon cilantro (coriander) seeds
1/2 teaspoon turmeric powder
1/2 teaspoon red chili powder
1/2 teaspoon garam masala
Salt to taste
Vegetable oil for frying

1. Mix all-purpose flour, salt, and vegetable oil until it forms breadcrumb texture.
2. Gradually add water, knead into stiff dough, then rest for 15-20 mins. In a pan, sauté cumin seeds, coriander seeds, onions, chilies, and ginger-garlic paste until fragrant.
3. Add spices, potatoes, and peas, cooking until well mixed.
4. Divide dough into balls, roll into circles, and halve.
5. Fill each half with potato mix, seal edges, and fry until crisp.
6. Drain excess oil, and serve hot.

Pakora

PREP: *15 Mins* **COOK:** *20 Mins* **Servings:** *4*

1 cup chickpea flour (besan) (120 grams)
1/2 teaspoon turmeric powder
1/2 teaspoon red chili powder
1/2 teaspoon cumin seeds
Salt to taste
Water as needed
Vegetable oil for frying
4 oz (100g) Sliced onions, spinach leaves, or sliced potatoes for pakoras

1. Mix chickpea flour, turmeric powder, red chili powder, cumin seeds, and salt in a mixing bowl.
2. Gradually add water and whisk to make a smooth batter. The consistency should be thick enough to coat the vegetables.
3. Put the deep frying pan or kadai over medium heat.
4. Dip the sliced onions, spinach leaves, or potatoes into the batter, ensuring they are coated well.
5. Gently drop the coated vegetables into the hot oil until crispy.
6. Remove the pakoras from the oil and drain on a paper towel to get out the excess oil.
7. Serve hot.

Pani Puri

PREP: *30 Mins* **COOK:** *20 Mins* **Servings:** *4*

Puris:
1 cup semolina (160g)
¼ cup all-purpose flour (30g)
Salt and Water as needed
Vegetable oil for frying

Pani (Spiced Water):
½ cup (15g) mint leaves
½ cup (15g) cilantro (coriander) leaves
2 green chilies, finely chopped
1-inch piece of ginger, grated
1 tsp cumin powder
1/4 tsp black pepper powder
1 tablespoon tamarind pulp
2 tablespoons lemon juice

Filling:
1 cup boiled and mashed potatoes (150 grams)
½ cup boiled and sprouted moong beans (80 grams)
1 small onion, finely chopped

1. Combine semolina, flour, and salt, knead into a stiff dough with water.
2. Rest for 20 mins, then roll into small thin circles. Fry these puris until golden, drain excess oil.
3. Blend mint, coriander, chilies, ginger into a paste, mix with cumin, chaat masala, black salt, black pepper, tamarind pulp, lemon juice, and water. Adjust taste and chill.
4. To assemble, make a hole in each puri, fill with potatoes, moong beans, and onions.
5. Serve with spiced water, tamarind and mint chutney. To eat, dip filled puri into water and enjoy.

Bhel Puri

PREP: *15 Mins* **COOK:** *5 Mins* **Servings:** *4*

3 cups puffed rice (murmura) (90 grams)
1 cup sev (thin crispy noodles) (80 grams)
½ cup finely chopped onions (80 grams)
½ cup finely chopped tomatoes (80 grams)
¼ cup finely chopped cucumber (40 grams)
¼ cup finely chopped raw mango (optional) (40 grams)
2 tablespoons finely chopped cilantro (coriander) leaves
2 tablespoons tamarind chutney
2 tablespoons mint chutney
1 tablespoon chaat masala
½ teaspoon red chili powder
Salt to taste
Lemon wedges (for serving)

1. In a bowl, combine puffed rice with sev, chopped onions, chopped tomatoes, chopped cucumber, chopped raw mango (if using), and chopped coriander leaves.
2. Add tamarind chutney, mint chutney, chaat masala, red chili powder (if using), and salt. Mix well to coat all the ingredients with the chutneys and spices.
3. Taste and adjust the seasonings if needed.
4. Serve immediately in individual bowls or plates, garnished with a sprinkle of sev and coriander leaves.
5. Squeeze some lemon juice over the bhel puri just before eating for an extra tangy flavor.

Vada Pav

PREP: *20 Mins* **COOK:** *20 Mins* **Servings:** *4*

Vada (Potato Filling):
4 large potatoes, boiled and mashed (400 grams)
2 green chilies, finely chopped
1 teaspoon ginger-garlic paste
½ teaspoon mustard seeds
½ teaspoon cumin seeds
½ teaspoon turmeric powder
½ teaspoon red chili powder
Salt to taste
Vegetable oil for frying
Pav (Buns):
4 pav buns (or burger buns)
Butter for toasting
For Serving:
Tamarind chutney
Mint chutney
Dry garlic chutney (optional)
Thinly sliced onions (optional)

1. **Vada:** In a pan with heated oil, splutter mustard and cumin seeds, then add green chilies and ginger-garlic paste. Stir in turmeric, red chili powder, salt, and mashed potatoes. After cooling slightly, shape into patties and fry till golden.
2. **Pav:** Half cut the buns and toast the insides with butter on a heated pan.
3. **To Assemble:** Inside each bun, spread tamarind and mint chutneys, sprinkle dry garlic chutney, and place a potato vada. Optionally, top with thinly sliced onions. Serve hot with additional chutneys.

Dahi Vada

PREP: *30 Mins* **COOK:** *20 Mins* **Servings:** *4*

Vada:
1 cup urad dal (split black lentils) (200 grams)
¼ cup moong dal (split yellow lentils) (50 grams)
2 green chilies, finely chopped
½-inch ginger, grated
Salt to taste
Vegetable oil for frying

Dahi (Yogurt Mixture):
2 cups thick yogurt (480 grams)
¼ cup milk (60 grams)
½ tsp roasted cumin powder
½ teaspoon red chili powder
¼ teaspoon black salt

Serving:
Tamarind or mint chutney
Roasted cumin powder
Red chili powder
Chopped cilantro (coriander) leaves

1. **Vada:** Soak urad and moong dal for 4-5 hrs, then grind to a paste. Add chilies, ginger, and salt. Wet hands, shape batter into round vadas, deep fry till crispy.
2. **Dahi:** Whisk yogurt, milk, cumin, chili powder, black salt, and salt until smooth.
3. **Assemble:** Soak fried vadas in water till soft. Squeeze out water, place in dish. Cover vadas with yogurt mixture, top with tamarind and mint chutney. Garnish with cumin, chili powder, and cilantro (coriander). Serve chilled.

Kachori

PREP: *30 Mins* **COOK:** *20 Mins* **Servings:** *4*

Dough:
2 cups all-purpose flour (240 grams)
¼ cup ghee or vegetable oil
Salt to taste
Water as needed
Filling:
1 cup green peas, coarsely ground (150 grams)
½ cup finely chopped onions
½ cup soaked and drained yellow moong dal (100 grams)
1 teaspoon ginger-garlic paste
1 teaspoon fennel seeds
1 teaspoon cumin seeds
1 teaspoon cilantro (coriander) powder
½ teaspoon turmeric powder
½ teaspoon red chili powder
½ teaspoon garam masala
Salt to taste
Vegetable oil for frying

1. **Dough:** Mix flour, ghee/oil, and salt. Add water gradually to knead a stiff dough. Rest for 15-20 mins.
2. **Filling:** Heat oil; splutter fennel and cumin seeds. Sauté onions till translucent, add ginger-garlic paste, then cook till fragrant. Mix in ground green peas, soaked moong dal, spices, and salt. Cook for 5-7 mins.
3. **Assemble:** Divide dough into balls, roll each into a circle. Add filling at the center, bring edges together, seal tightly. Deep fry until crispy. Serve hot.

Chole Bhature

PREP: *15 Mins* **COOK:** *1 hour* **Servings:** *4*

Chole:

2 cups chickpeas (garbazo beans), soaked overnight
1 onion, finely chopped
2 tomatoes, pureed
2 tsp ginger-garlic paste
2 tsp chole masala
1 tsp turmeric powder
Salt to taste
2 tbsp oil

Bhature:

2 cups all-purpose flour
1/2 cup yogurt
1 tsp baking powder
Salt to taste
Oil for frying

Chole:

1. Pressure cook soaked chickpeas until soft. Heat oil in a pan, sauté onions until golden.
2. Add ginger-garlic paste, tomato puree, chole masala, turmeric, and salt. Cook until oil separates.
3. Add cooked chickpeas, simmer for 10 minutes.

Bhature:

4. Mix flour, yogurt, baking powder, and salt. Knead into a soft dough.
5. Divide into small balls and roll into discs.
6. Heat oil in a pan and deep-fry discs until puffed and golden.
7. Serve hot chole with bhature. Enjoy!

Aloo Tikki

PREP: *20 Mins* **COOK:** *15 Mins* **Servings:** *4*

4 medium potatoes, boiled and mashed (400 grams)
¼ cup breadcrumbs (30 grams)
¼ cup finely chopped onions (40 grams)
¼ cup boiled and mashed green peas (40 grams)
2 tablespoons finely chopped cilantro (coriander) leaves
1 teaspoon ginger-garlic paste
1 teaspoon chaat masala
½ teaspoon red chili powder
½ teaspoon cumin powder
Salt to taste
Vegetable oil for shallow frying

1. Combine mashed potatoes, breadcrumbs, chopped onions, green peas, coriander leaves, ginger-garlic paste, chaat masala, red chili, and cumin powder with salt in a mixing bowl. Mix well to form a cohesive mixture.
2. Divide the mixture into equal-sized portions and shape each into a round or flattened tikki.
3. Heat oil in a non-stick skillet or griddle over medium heat.
4. Place the tikkis on the hot skillet and shallow fry them until golden brown and crispy on both sides.
5. Remove the tikkis from the skillet and drain to remove excess oil.
6. Serve hot.

MAIN COURSES VEGETARIAN

Palak Paneer

PREP: *20 Mins* **COOK:** *30 Mins* **Servings:** *4*

2 bunches of fresh spinach (about 500 grams)
7 oz. (200 grams) paneer, cubed
1 large onion, finely chopped
2 tomatoes, finely chopped
2 green chilies, slit
1 teaspoon ginger-garlic paste
1 teaspoon cumin seeds
1/2 teaspoon turmeric powder
1/2 teaspoon red chili powder
1/2 teaspoon garam masala
Salt to taste
2 tablespoons ghee or vegetable oil

1. Wash the spinach leaves thoroughly and blanch them in boiling water for 2 minutes. Drain and rinse with cold water to retain the vibrant green color.
2. Blend the spinach into a smooth puree. Set aside. Heat ghee or vegetable oil in a pan. Add cumin seeds and let them splutter. Add finely chopped onions and sauté until they turn golden brown.
3. Add 1 tsp ginger-garlic paste and cook for a minute until fragrant. Add tomatoes and slit green chilies. Cook until the tomatoes are softened. Add turmeric powder, red chili powder, garam masala, and salt. Mix well.
4. Pour in blended spinach and mix everything. Cook for 5-7 minutes on medium heat. Add cubed paneer and stir gently to coat. Cook for another 5 minutes. Remove from heat, cool a bit, and serve hot with roti, naan, or rice.

Chana Masala

PREP: *10 Mins* **COOK:** *30 Mins* **Servings:** *4*

2 cups cooked chickpeas (garbazo beans) (400 grams)
2 medium onions, finely chopped
2 tomatoes, finely chopped
2 green chilies, slit
1 teaspoon ginger-garlic paste
1 teaspoon cumin seeds
1 teaspoon cilantro (coriander) powder
1/2 teaspoon turmeric powder
1/2 teaspoon red chili powder
1/2 teaspoon garam masala
Salt to taste
2 tablespoons vegetable oil
Fresh cilantro (coriander) leaves for garnish

1. Heat vegetable oil in a pan. Add cumin seeds and let them splutter. Add finely chopped onions and sauté until they turn golden brown.
2. Add 1 tsp ginger-garlic paste and cook for a minute until fragrant. Add finely chopped tomatoes and slit green chilies. Cook until the tomatoes are softened.
3. Add coriander, turmeric, red chili, garam masala, and salt. Mix well. Cook the masala on medium heat for a few minutes until the oil separates from the mixture.
4. Add cooked chickpeas and mix well to coat them with the masala. Add water as needed to adjust the consistency of the gravy. Simmer for 13-15 minutes to allow the flavors to meld together.
5. Garnish with fresh coriander leaves. Serve hot with roti, naan, or rice.

Aloo Gobi

PREP: *15 Mins* **COOK:** *25 Mins* **Servings:** *4*

1 medium cauliflower, cut into florets
2 medium potatoes, peeled and cubed
1 large onion, finely chopped
2 tomatoes, finely chopped
1 teaspoon ginger-garlic paste
1 teaspoon cumin seeds
1 teaspoon cilantro (coriander) powder
1/2 teaspoon turmeric powder
1/2 teaspoon red chili powder
1/2 teaspoon garam masala
Salt to taste
2 tablespoons vegetable oil
Fresh cilantro (coriander) leaves for garnish

1. Heat vegetable oil in a pan. Add cumin seeds and let them splutter. Add finely chopped onions and sauté until they turn golden brown.
2. Add 1 tsp ginger-garlic paste and cook for one minute until fragrant. Add finely chopped tomatoes and cook until they are soft and mushy.
3. Add coriander, turmeric, red chili, garam masala, and salt. Mix well. Add cubed potatoes and cauliflower florets. Mix everything to coat them with the masala.
4. Cook on medium heat for a few minutes, then cover and cook for 17-20 minutes until the vegetables are tender.
5. Stir occasionally to prevent sticking. Garnish with fresh coriander leaves. Serve hot with roti, naan, or rice.

Rajma with Rice

PREP: *8 Hour* **COOK:** *1 Hour* **Servings:** *4*

Rajma (Kidney Bean Curry):
1 cup rajma (red kidney beans) (200g), soaked overnight and drained
2 tablespoons oil or ghee
1 large onion, finely chopped
2 tomatoes, finely chopped
1 tablespoon ginger-garlic paste
1 teaspoon cumin seeds
1 teaspoon cilantro (coriander) powder
1/2 teaspoon turmeric powder
1/2 teaspoon red chili powder
1/2 teaspoon garam masala
Salt to taste
Water as needed

Rice:
1 cup basmati rice (200 grams)
2 cups water

1. Boil rajma with water and salt until tender. Heat oil in a pan, add cumin seeds, onions, and sauté until golden. Add ginger-garlic paste, followed by tomatoes. Add spices and the cooked rajma, simmer for about 40 minutes.
2. Rinse basmati rice until clear, then boil it with water. Lower the heat, cover, and simmer until rice is cooked.
3. Serve rajma curry over cooked rice. Garnish with coriander, if desired, and serve hot with salad or raita.

Baingan Bharta

PREP: *10 Mins* **COOK:** *30 Mins* **Servings:** *4*

2 large eggplants (baingan) (aubergine)
2 tablespoons oil
1 large onion, finely chopped
2 tomatoes, finely chopped
2 green chilies, finely chopped
1 tablespoon ginger-garlic paste
1/2 teaspoon cumin seeds
1/2 teaspoon turmeric powder
1/2 teaspoon red chili powder
1/2 teaspoon cilantro (coriander) powder
Salt to taste
Fresh cilantro (coriander) leaves for garnish

Roast Eggplants:

1. Preheat oven to 400°F (200°C), pierce eggplants, and place on a baking sheet. Roast for about 30 minutes until skin is charred and flesh is soft. Let them cool, remove charred skin, and mash the flesh.

Prepare Bharta:

2. Heat oil in a pan, add cumin seeds and onions, sauté until golden. Add ginger-garlic paste, followed by tomatoes and green chilies. Once tomatoes are soft, add spices and mashed eggplant. Cook for 13-15 minutes, stirring occasionally.
3. Adjust seasoning if needed, garnish with coriander, and serve hot with roti, naan, or rice.

Dal Tadka

PREP: *5 Mins* **COOK:** *30 Mins* **Servings:** *4*

1 cup yellow lentils (toor dal), rinsed and drained (200 grams)
3 cups water (750g)
1 medium onion, finely chopped
2 tomatoes, finely chopped
2 green chilies, slit
1 teaspoon ginger-garlic paste
1/2 teaspoon turmeric powder
1/2 teaspoon red chili powder
1/2 teaspoon cumin seeds
1/2 teaspoon mustard seeds
1/2 teaspoon asafoetida (hing)
1 tablespoon ghee or vegetable oil
Salt to taste
Fresh cilantro (coriander) leaves for garnish

1. In a pressure cooker, cook toor dal with water for 4-5 whistles. Heat ghee or vegetable oil in a pan, add cumin and mustard seeds.
2. Once they splutter, add onions, ginger-garlic paste, tomatoes, and green chilies. Cook until tomatoes are mushy, then add spices.
3. Stir in the cooked dal and simmer for 13-15 minutes. Adjust seasoning, garnish with coriander leaves, and serve hot with rice or roti.

Bhindi Masala

PREP: *10 Mins* **COOK:** *20 Mins* **Servings:** *4*

1.1 lb. (500 grams) bhindi (okra), washed and dried
2 tablespoons oil
1 large onion, finely chopped
2 tomatoes, finely chopped
1 teaspoon ginger-garlic paste
1 teaspoon cumin seeds
1 teaspoon cilantro (coriander) powder
½ teaspoon turmeric powder
½ teaspoon red chili powder
½ teaspoon garam masala
Salt to taste
Fresh coriander leaves for garnish

1. Trim the ends of the bhindi and slice them into 1-inch pieces.
2. Heat oil in a pan. Add cumin seeds and let them splutter.
3. Add chopped onions and sauté until they turn golden brown.
4. Add 1 tsp ginger-garlic paste and cook for a minute until fragrant.
5. Add chopped tomatoes and cook until mushy. Add coriander, turmeric, red chili, garam masala, and salt. Mix well.
6. Add the sliced bhindi and stir everything together to coat the bhindi with the masala. Cook on medium heat for 17-20 minutes, stirring occasionally, until the bhindi is cooked and tender.
7. Garnish with fresh coriander leaves.
8. Serve hot with roti or rice.

Paneer Butter Masala

PREP: *15 Mins* **COOK:** *30 Mins* **Servings:** *4*

7 oz (200 grams) paneer, cubed
2 tablespoons butter
1 large onion, finely chopped
2 tomatoes, finely chopped
1 teaspoon ginger-garlic paste
1 teaspoon cumin seeds
1 teaspoon cilantro (coriander) powder
½ teaspoon turmeric powder
½ teaspoon red chili powder
½ teaspoon garam masala
¼ cup (35 grams) cashew nuts, soaked in warm water for 15 minutes
¼ cup milk (60 grams)
Salt to taste
Fresh cream for garnish
Fresh cilantro (coriander) leaves for garnish

1. Heat butter in a pan. Add cumin seeds and let them splutter. Add chopped onions and sauté until they turn golden brown.
2. Add 1 tsp ginger-garlic paste and cook for a minute until fragrant.
3. Put in chopped tomatoes and cook until they are softened and mushy. Add coriander, turmeric, red chili, garam masala, and salt. Mix well.
4. Blend the soaked cashew nuts with milk to make a smooth paste.
5. Add cashew paste to the pan and mix everything. Add the cubed paneer and stir gently to coat it with the masala.
6. Cook on medium heat for 13-15 minutes, stirring occasionally, to allow the flavors to meld together.
7. Garnish with fresh cream and fresh coriander leaves. Serve hot with naan, roti, or rice.

Matar Paneer

PREP: *15Mins* **COOK:** *30 Mins* **Servings:** *4*

7 oz (200 grams) paneer, cubed
1 cup green peas, fresh or frozen (150 grams)
2 tablespoons oil
1 large onion, finely chopped
2 tomatoes, finely chopped
1 teaspoon ginger-garlic paste
1 teaspoon cumin seeds
1 teaspoon cilantro (coriander) powder
1/2 teaspoon turmeric powder
1/2 teaspoon red chili powder
1/2 teaspoon garam masala
Salt to taste
Fresh cilantro (coriander) leaves for garnish

1. Heat oil in a pan. Add cumin seeds and let them splutter.
2. Add chopped onions and sauté until they turn golden brown.
3. Add 1 tsp ginger-garlic paste and cook for a minute until fragrant.
4. Add chopped tomatoes and cook until softened and mushy.
5. Add coriander, turmeric, red chili, garam masala, and salt. Mix well.
6. Add the green peas and cubed paneer. Stir everything together to coat the peas and paneer with the masala.
7. Cook on medium heat for 13-15 minutes, stirring occasionally, until the peas are cooked and the paneer is heated.
8. Garnish with fresh coriander leaves.
9. Serve hot with roti, naan, or rice.

Dal Makhani

PREP: *8 Hour* **COOK:** *90 Mins* **Servings:** *4*

1 cup whole black lentils (sabut urad dal), soaked overnight and drained (200 grams)
¼ cup kidney beans (rajma), soaked overnight and drained (50 grams)
4 cups water (1 liter)
2 tablespoons butter
1 tablespoon oil
1 large onion, finely chopped
2 tomatoes, finely chopped
1 tablespoon ginger-garlic paste
1 teaspoon cumin seeds
1 tsp cilantro (coriander) powder
½ teaspoon turmeric powder
½ teaspoon red chili powder
½ teaspoon garam masala
¼ cup heavy cream
Salt to taste
Fresh coriander leaves

1. Combine soaked and drained whole black lentils, kidney beans, and 4 cups of water in a pressure cooker. Pressure cook for 5-6 whistles or until the lentils and beans are soft and cooked. Set aside.
2. Heat butter and oil in a pan. Add cumin seeds and let them splutter. Add chopped onions and sauté until they turn golden brown. Add 1 tsp ginger-garlic paste and cook for a minute until fragrant.
3. Add chopped tomatoes and cook soft and mushy. Add coriander, turmeric, red chili, garam masala, and salt. Mix well.
4. Add the cooked lentils and beans along with their water. Stir everything together.
5. Simmer the dal makhani on low heat for 1 hour, stirring occasionally. Mash the dal slightly with the back of a spoon to thicken the gravy. Stir in the heavy cream, whisk well, and cook for 10 minutes. Garnish with fresh coriander leaves. Serve hot with naan, roti, or rice.

Kadai Paneer

PREP: *15 Mins* **COOK:** *25 Mins* **Servings:** *4*

7 oz. (200 grams) paneer, cubed
2 tablespoons oil
1 large onion, finely chopped
1 large bell pepper (capsicum), cut into cubes
2 tomatoes, finely chopped
1 tablespoon ginger-garlic paste
2 green chilies, slit
1 teaspoon cumin seeds
1 teaspoon cilantro (coriander) powder
1/2 teaspoon turmeric powder
1/2 teaspoon red chili powder
1/2 teaspoon garam masala
Salt to taste
Fresh cilantro (coriander) leaves for garnish

1. Heat oil in a pan/kadai. Add cumin seeds and let them splutter. Add chopped onions and sauté until they turn golden brown. Add 1 tsp ginger-garlic paste and cook for a minute until fragrant.
2. Add slit green chilies and bell pepper cubes. Cook for three minutes until the bell peppers are slightly tender. Put in chopped tomatoes and cook until they are soft and mushy.
3. Add coriander, turmeric, red chili, garam masala, and salt. Mix well. Add the cubed paneer and stir gently to coat it with the masala.
4. Cook on moderate heat for 5-7 minutes, stirring occasionally, until the paneer is heated and the flavors are well combined. Garnish with fresh coriander leaves. Serve hot with naan, roti, or rice.

MAIN COURSES NON VEGETARIAN

Butter Chicken

PREP: *2 Hrs 15 Mins* **COOK:** *30 Mins* **Servings:** *4*

1 lb. (450 grams) of boneless chicken cut into pieces
1 tablespoon lemon juice
1 teaspoon red chili powder
Salt to taste
½ cup (113 grams) unsalted butter
2 tablespoons ginger garlic paste
1 lb. (450 grams) tomato puree
1 cup (240 ml) heavy cream
1 tablespoon sugar
1 tablespoon dried fenugreek leaves (Kasuri methi)

1. Marinate the chicken pieces with lemon juice, red chili powder, and salt. Set aside for about 2 hours.
2. Heat 1/2 cup butter in a non-stick pan, add the ginger garlic paste, and sauté until the raw smell disappears.
3. Add the tomato puree, sugar, and marinated chicken and cook until the chicken is done.
4. Add the heavy cream and kasuri methi, stir well, and cook for a few more minutes.
5. Serve hot with naan or rice.

Chicken Tikka Masala

PREP: *2 hrs 20 Mins* **COOK:** *40 Mins* **Servings:** *4*

- 1 lb. (450 grams) of boneless chicken cut into pieces
- 1 cup (240 ml) plain yogurt
- 2 tablespoons ginger garlic paste
- 1 tablespoon garam masala
- Salt to taste
- 2 tablespoons vegetable oil
- 3 cups (150 grams) onion, finely chopped
- 1 tablespoon ground cilantro (coriander)
- 1 teaspoon ground cumin
- 1 teaspoon turmeric
- 1 teaspoon red chili powder
- 1 cup heavy cream
- 1 lb. (450 grams) tomato puree
- Fresh coriander leaves for garnish

1. Marinate the chicken pieces with yogurt, ginger garlic paste, garam masala, and salt. Set aside for about 2 hours.
2. Heat two oil in a pan, add the onions, and sauté until golden.
3. Add the ground coriander, cumin, turmeric, and red chili powder.
4. Add the marinated chicken and cook until it's fully cooked.
5. Add tomato puree and heavy cream, stir well, and simmer for 15 minutes.
6. Decorate with coriander leaves and serve hot with naan or rice.

Mutton Korma

PREP: *30 Mins* **COOK:** *90 Mins* **Servings:** *4*

1.1 lb. (500 grams) mutton, cut into pieces
2 tablespoons vegetable oil
2 medium onions, finely chopped
2 teaspoons ginger-garlic paste
2 green chilies, slit
1 teaspoon turmeric powder
1 teaspoon red chili powder
1 teaspoon cilantro (coriander) powder
½ teaspoon garam masala
Salt to taste
1 cup plain yogurt (240g) (or dairy-free alternative), whisked
1 cup water (240 ml)
Fresh coriander leaves, chopped (for garnish)

1. Heat oil in a large pan or pressure cooker. Add diced onions and sauté until golden brown. Add ginger-garlic paste and green chilies. Cook for a minute until the raw aroma disappears. Add mutton pieces and cook until they are browned on all sides. Add turmeric powder, red chili powder, coriander powder, garam masala, and salt. Mix well to coat the mutton with the spices.
2. Add whisked yogurt (or a dairy-free alternative) and cook for a few minutes, stirring continuously.
3. If using a pressure cooker, add water and pressure cook for 30-40 minutes until the mutton is tender. If using a regular pan, add water, cover, and simmer for 1-1.5 hours or until the mutton is tender, stirring occasionally and adding more water if needed.
4. Once the mutton is cooked and the gravy has thickened, garnish with fresh coriander leaves. Serve hot with naan, roti, or rice.

Chicken Biryani

PREP: *30 Mins* **COOK:** *1 Hour* **Servings:** *4*

Salt to taste
2 tablespoons vegetable oil
3 cups (150 grams) onion, finely chopped
1 lb. (450 grams) of boneless chicken cut into pieces
1 cup (240 ml) plain yogurt
1 tablespoon garam masala
2 tablespoons ginger garlic paste
1 teaspoon turmeric
1 teaspoon red chili powder
1 lb. (450 grams) basmati rice
1-liter water
Fresh cilantro (coriander) leaves for garnish

1. Marinate the chicken pieces with yogurt, garam masala, and salt. Set aside for about 2 hours.
2. Heat two tbsp oil in a large pot, add the onions, and sauté until golden.
3. Add ginger garlic paste, turmeric, and red chili powder to the pot and stir well.
4. Add the marinated chicken and cook until it's fully cooked.
5. In another pot, cook basmati rice in boiling water until it's 70% cooked. Drain the water.
6. Layer the partially cooked rice over the chicken in the pot. Cover and cook on low heat for about 27-30 minutes, until the rice is fully cooked and flavors have melded together.
7. Top with coriander leaves and serve hot.

Fish Curry

PREP: *10 Mins* **COOK:** *30 Mins* **Servings:** *4*

1 lb. (450 grams) fish, cut into pieces
2 tablespoons vegetable oil
1 tablespoon cilantro (coriander) powder
1 lb. (450 grams) tomatoes, chopped
2 cups (500 ml) water
3 cups (150 grams) onion, finely chopped
2 tablespoons ginger garlic paste
1 teaspoon turmeric
1 teaspoon red chili powder
Salt to taste
Fresh cilantro (coriander) leaves for garnish

1. Heat two tbsp oil in a sauteeing pan, then add diced onions, and sauté until golden.
2. Add ginger garlic paste, turmeric, red chili powder, and coriander powder to the pan and stir well.
3. Add 450g tomatoes and cook until they are soft and mushy.
4. Add water and boil the mixture. Add fish pieces and cook until they are done.
5. Decorate with fresh coriander leaves and serve hot with rice.

Chicken Curry

PREP: *15 Mins* **COOK:** *45 Mins* **Servings:** *4*

1 lb. (500 grams) chicken, cut into pieces
2 tablespoons vegetable oil
1 teaspoon red chili powder
1 tablespoon cilantro (coriander) powder
1.1 lb. (500 grams) tomatoes, chopped
2 cups (500 ml) water
3 cups (150 grams) onion, finely chopped
2 tablespoons ginger garlic paste
1 teaspoon turmeric
Salt to taste
Fresh cilantro (coriander) leaves for garnish

1. Heat two tbsp oil, add the onions, and sauté until golden.
2. Add ginger garlic paste, turmeric, red chili powder, and coriander powder to the pan and stir well.
3. Add 1 lb tomatoes and cook until they are soft and mushy.
4. Add meat pieces and cook until they are done.
5. Add water, boil, and then simmer until the chicken is
6. done.
7. Decorate with coriander leaves and serve hot with rice or naan.

Malabar Fish Curry

PREP: *10 Mins* **COOK:** *30 Mins* **Servings:** *4*

1 lb. (450 grams) fish, cut into pieces
2 tablespoons vegetable oil
3 cups (150 grams) onion, finely chopped
2 tablespoons ginger garlic paste
1 teaspoon turmeric
1 teaspoon red chili powder
1 tablespoon coriander powder
1 lb. (450 grams) tomatoes, chopped
2 cups (500 ml) water
1 cup (240 ml) thick coconut milk
Salt to taste
Fresh cilantro (coriander) leaves for garnish

1. Heat oil in a sauteeing pan, add diced onions, and sauté until golden.
2. Add ginger garlic paste, turmeric, red chili powder, and coriander powder to the pan and stir well.
3. Add 1 lb tomatoes and cook until they are soft and mushy.
4. Add water and boil the mixture. Add fish pieces and cook until they are done.
5. Add coconut milk, whisk well, and simmer for a few minutes until the flavors meld together.
6. Decorate with chopped coriander leaves and serve hot with rice.

Keema Matar

PREP: *10 Mins* **COOK:** *30 Mins* **Servings:** *4*

1. lb. 450 grams minced mutton
2 tablespoons vegetable oil
3 cups (150 grams) onion, finely chopped
2 tablespoons ginger garlic paste
1 teaspoon turmeric
1 teaspoon red chili powder
1 tablespoon cilantro (coriander) powder
1.1 lb. (500 grams) tomatoes, chopped
2 cups (240 grams) of green peas
2 cups (500 ml) water
Salt to taste
Fresh cilantro (coriander) leaves for garnish

1. Heat oil in a sauteeing pan, add diced onions, and sauté until golden.
2. Add ginger garlic paste, turmeric, red chili powder, and coriander powder to the pan and stir well.
3. Add 500g tomatoes and cook until they are soft and mushy.
4. Add minced mutton and cook until it is browned and cooked through.
5. Add green peas, water, and salt, and simmer until the peas are cooked and the flavors have melded together.
6. Decorate with fresh coriander leaves and serve hot with rice or naan.

SIDE DISHES

Raita

PREP: *10 Mins* **COOK:** -- **Servings:** *4*

1 cup (240gram) plain yogurt
1 medium cucumber (peeled, seedless, and chopped)
Salt to taste
½ teaspoon cumin powder
Fresh cilantro (coriander) leaves for garnish

1. Combine yogurt, cucumber, salt, and cumin powder in a bowl and stir until well combined.
2. Refrigerate for at least 30 minutes before serving to allow flavors to blend.
3. Garnish with fresh coriander leaves and serve chilled.

Kachumber Salad

PREP: *10 Mins* **COOK:** -- **Servings:** *4*

1 medium cucumber, finely chopped
2 medium tomatoes, finely chopped
1 medium onion, finely chopped
1 green chili, finely chopped (optional)
Juice of 1 lemon
Salt to taste
Fresh cilantro (coriander) leaves, finely chopped

1. In a bowl, combine the finely chopped cucumber, tomatoes, onion, and green chili (if used).
2. Squeeze the juice of one lemon over the ingredients in the bowl. The lemon juice will add a tangy and refreshing flavor to the salad.
3. Sprinkle salt over the salad according to your taste preferences. Adjust the salt as needed.
4. To enhance the flavor and add a fresh aroma, finely chop some fresh coriander leaves and add them to the bowl.
5. Toss the all ingredients in the bowl well, ensuring they are mixed thoroughly. This will help the flavors combine.
6. The kachumber salad is now ready to be served. Serve it immediately as a side dish or accompaniment to your main meal.

Mango Pickle

PREP: *20 Mins* **REST TIME:** *2-3 days* **Servings:** *varies*

1.1 lb. (500 grams) raw mango, cut into pieces
½ cup (135 grams) salt
2 tablespoons red chili powder
1 tablespoon turmeric
2 tablespoons 30 ml mustard oil

1. Mix mango pieces with salt, chili powder, and turmeric in a large bowl.
2. Heat mustard oil to the smoking point, then allow it to cool completely.
3. Add cooled oil to the mango mixture and mix well.
4. Store in a sterilized jar, and let it rest for 2-3 days before using. Serve and enjoy.

Coconut Chutney

PREP: *10 Mins* **COOK:** -- **Servings:** *4*

1½ cups (150 grams) freshly grated coconut
2 green chilies
Salt to taste
1 cup (240 ml) water

1. Combine 150 grams of freshly grated coconut, 2 green chilies, and salt in a blender to taste.
2. Gradually add 240 ml of water while blending until a smooth paste forms.
3. Serve the coconut chutney immediately or refrigerate for later use.

Onion Tomato Salad

PREP: *10 Mins* **COOK:** -- **Servings:** *4*

2 medium onions, thinly sliced
2 medium tomatoes, thinly sliced
1 green chili, finely chopped (optional)
Juice of 1 lemon
Salt to taste
Fresh cilantro (coriander) leaves, finely chopped

1. Thinly slice 2 medium onions and 2 medium tomatoes, and finely chop 1 green chili (optional).
2. Combine the onions, tomatoes, green chili, 1 lemon juice, salt to taste, and freshly chopped coriander leaves in a bowl.
3. Toss the ingredients well and serve immediately.

Carrot Pickle

PREP: *15 Mins* **REST TIME:** *2-3 days* **Servings:** *Varies*

1.1 lb. (500 grams) carrots, cut into pieces
½ cup (135 grams) salt
2 tablespoons red chili powder
1 tablespoon turmeric
2 tablespoons (30 ml) mustard oil

1. Mix carrot pieces with salt, chili powder, and turmeric in a large bowl.
2. Heat mustard oil to the smoking point, then allow it to cool completely.
3. Add the cooled oil to the carrot mixture and mix well.
4. Store in a sterilized jar, and let it rest for 2-3 days before using. Serve and enjoy.

Lime Pickle

PREP: *20 Mins* **REST TIME:** *2-3 days* **Servings:** *varies*

1.1 lb. (500 grams) limes, cut into wedges
½ cup (135 grams) salt
2 tablespoons red chili powder
1 tablespoon turmeric
2 tablespoons mustard oil

1. Mix lime wedges with salt, chili powder, and turmeric in a large bowl.
2. Heat mustard oil to the smoking point, then allow it to cool completely.
3. Add the cooled oil to the lime mixture and mix well.
4. Store in a sterilized jar, and let it rest for 2-3 days before using. Serve and enjoy.

Green Chili Pickle

PREP: *15 Mins* **REST TIME:** *2-3 days* **Servings:** *Varies*

1.1 lb. (500 grams) of green chilies, cut into pieces
½ cup (135 grams) salt
2 tablespoons red chili powder
1 tablespoon turmeric
2 tablespoon mustard oil

1. Mix green chili pieces with salt, chili powder, and turmeric in a large bowl.
2. Heat mustard oil to the smoking point, then allow it to cool completely.
3. Add the cooled oil to the chili mixture and mix well.
4. Store in a sterilized jar, and let it rest for 2-3 days before using. Serve and enjoy

Indian Roti

PREP: *20 Mins* **COOK:** *15 Mins* **Servings:** *4*

2 cups whole wheat flour
1/2 tsp salt
3/4 to 1 cup warm water

1. In a mixing bowl, combine whole wheat flour and salt.
2. Slowly add warm water and knead the dough until it becomes smooth and soft. Adjust the water as needed; you may not need the full cup.
3. Cover the dough with a damp cloth and let it rest for 15-20 minutes.
4. Divide the dough into small balls, about the size of a golf ball.
5. On a floured surface, roll each ball into a thin circle using a rolling pin.
6. Heat a flat skillet or tava over medium heat.
7. Place a rolled roti on the hot skillet and cook for about 1 minute or until bubbles start to form.
8. Flip the roti and cook the other side for another minute until it puffs up and gets brown spots.

Garlic Naan

PREP: *20 Mins* **COOK:** *10 Mins* **Servings:** *4*

2 cups all-purpose flour
1 tsp sugar
1/2 tsp baking powder
1/4 tsp baking soda
1/2 tsp salt
1/2 cup warm water
1/4 cup plain yogurt
2 tbsp vegetable oil
4 cloves garlic, minced
2 tbsp vegan butter or ghee (melted, for brushing)
Fresh cilantro (cilantro (coriander)) leaves for garnish

1. Mix dry ingredients in a bowl. Combine water, yogurt, and oil in another bowl.
2. Gradually add wet ingredients to dry, knead into a smooth dough. Let dough rest for 1 hour. Divide and flatten dough, roll into ovals or rounds.
3. Sprinkle garlic over naan.
4. Cook naan in a preheated skillet until puffed and golden.
5. Brush with melted butter/ghee, garnish with cilantro.

PUNJAB SPECIALTIES

Sarson da Saag with Makki di Roti

PREP: *20 Mins* **COOK:** *1 Hour* **Servings:** *4*

14 oz. (400 grams) mustard greens
7 oz. (200 grams) spinach
2 green chilies
1 tablespoon ginger
1 tablespoon garlic
2 tablespoons ghee (clarified butter)
Salt to taste
1 teaspoon turmeric powder
1 teaspoon red chili powder
7 oz. (200 grams) cornmeal

1. Clean and wash the mustard greens and spinach. Chop them roughly with green chilies, ginger, and garlic.
2. Boil these greens with a cup of water until they become soft. Cool and blend into a smooth paste.
3. Heat 2 tbsp ghee in a non-stick pan; add the green paste, salt, turmeric, and red chili powder. Cook on a low flame for about half an hour.
4. Meanwhile, prepare the roti by mixing cornmeal with water and kneading it into a soft dough. Roll into flatbreads and cook on a hot grill until golden brown on both sides.
5. Serve the saag hot with a dollop of butter, accompanied by the makki di roti.

Amritsari Chole

PREP: *15 Mins* **COOK:** *1 Hour* **Servings:** *4*

7 oz. (200 grams) chickpeas (garbazo beans)
2 tablespoons oil
2 onions, chopped
1 tablespoon ginger-garlic paste
2 tomatoes, pureed
2 green chilies, slit
1 teaspoon cumin seeds
1 teaspoon turmeric powder
1 teaspoon red chili powder
1 teaspoon garam masala
Salt to taste
Fresh cilantro (cilantro (coriander))
leaves, for garnish

1. Soak the chickpeas overnight; then pressure cook them until soft.
2. Heat oil (two tbsp) in a pan and add cumin seeds. When they look to crackle, add onions and sauté until golden brown.
3. Add the ginger-garlic paste and green chilies, followed by the pureed tomatoes. Cook until the oil completely separates from the masala.
4. Add the boiled chickpeas, turmeric, red chili powder, garam masala, and salt. Simmer for 15-20 minutes.
5. Decorate with fresh coriander leaves and serve hot with rice or roti.

Punjabi Kadhi Pakora

PREP: *20 Mins* **COOK:** *1 Hour* **Servings:** *4*

7 oz. (200 grams) gram flour
18 oz. (500 grams) yogurt
2 onions, chopped
1 teaspoon fenugreek seeds
1 teaspoon cumin seeds
1 teaspoon turmeric powder
1 teaspoon red chili powder
Salt to taste
2 tablespoons oil
Fresh cilantro (coriander) leaves, for garnish

1. Mix half the gram flour with a little water to make a thick batter. Place spoonfuls of batter into hot oil and fry until golden brown. Drain and keep aside.
2. In a separate bowl, whisk the yogurt with the remaining gram flour, turmeric, and a little water until smooth.
3. Heat oil (two tbsp) in a non-stick pan and add fenugreek and cumin seeds. When they look to crackle, add onions and sauté until golden brown.
4. Add the yogurt mixture and salt. Bring to a boil, then simmer for about half an hour until the kadhi thickens.
5. Add the pakoras to the khadi and simmer for another 10 minutes.
6. Decorate with fresh coriander leaves and serve hot with rice.

Pindi Chole

PREP: *15 Mins* **COOK:** *1 Hour* **Servings:** *4*

7 oz. (200 grams) chickpeas (garbazo beans)
2 tablespoons oil
2 onions, chopped
1 tablespoon ginger-garlic paste
2 tomatoes, pureed
1 teaspoon cumin seeds
1 teaspoon turmeric powder
1 teaspoon red chili powder
1 teaspoon garam masala
Salt to taste
Fresh cilantro (coriander) leaves, for garnish

1. Soak the chickpeas overnight; then pressure cook them until soft.
2. Heat oil in a pan; once hot, then add cumin seeds. When they crackle thoroughly, add onions and sauté until golden brown.
3. Add the ginger-garlic paste, followed by the pureed tomatoes. Cook until the oil completely separates from the masala.
4. Add the boiled chickpeas, turmeric, red chili powder, garam masala, and salt. Simmer for 15-20 minutes.
5. Decorate with fresh coriander leaves and serve hot with rice or roti.

SOUTH INDIAN SPECIALITIES

Avial

PREP: *20 Mins* **COOK:** *30 Mins* **Servings:** *4*

4 cups (400g) mixed vegetables (carrot, beans, drumstick, potato, etc.)
1 cup (100g) grated coconut
2 green chilies
1 teaspoon cumin seeds
1/2 cup (120ml) yogurt
Salt to taste
1 tablespoon coconut oil
Few curry leaves

1. Boil the vegetables with salt and a little water until they are soft.
2. Grind the coconut with green chilies and cumin seeds into a coarse paste.
3. Add this paste to the boiled vegetables, followed by the yogurt. Mix well.
4. Heat the coconut oil and add curry leaves. Pour this tempering over the Avial.
5. Serve hot with rice.

Sambar

PREP: *15 Mins* **COOK:** *30 Mins* **Servings:** *4*

- 1 cup (200g) pigeon peas (toor dal)
- 2 cups (200g) mixed vegetables (okra, carrot, drumstick, etc.)
- 1 tablespoon sambar powder
- 1 teaspoon turmeric powder
- Salt to taste
- 1 tablespoon tamarind paste
- 2 tablespoons oil
- 1 teaspoon mustard seeds
- Few curry leaves

1. Pressure-cook the pigeon peas with turmeric powder until they are soft.
2. Boil the vegetables with salt and sambar powder. Add the tamarind paste and cooked pigeon peas.
3. Simmer for a few minutes until the flavors blend.
4. Heat the oil and add mustard seeds. When they crackle thoroughly, add curry leaves.
5. Pour this tempering over the sambar and serve hot with rice.

Rasam

PREP: *20 Mins* **COOK:** *20 Mins* **Servings:** *4*

2 tomatoes, chopped
1 teaspoon tamarind paste
1 teaspoon rasam powder
Salt to taste
2 cups (500ml) water
2 tablespoons oil
1 teaspoon mustard seeds
1 teaspoon cumin seeds
Few curry leaves

1. Boil the tomatoes with tamarind paste, rasam powder, salt, and water.
2. Simmer for a few minutes until the flavors blend.
3. Heat the oil; once hot, then mustard seeds and cumin seeds. When they crackle thoroughly, add curry leaves.
4. Pour this tempering over the rasam and serve hot with rice.

Lemon Rice

PREP: *10 Mins* **COOK:** *20 Mins* **Servings:** *4*

2 cups (400g) cooked rice
Juice of 2 lemons
Salt to taste
2 tablespoons oil
1 teaspoon mustard seeds
1 teaspoon turmeric powder
Few curry leaves
2 red chilies
1/4 cup (40g) peanuts

1. Heat the oil and add mustard seeds. Add turmeric powder, curry leaves, red chilies, and peanuts when they begin to crackle.
2. Add the cooked rice, lemon juice, and salt. Mix well.
3. Serve the lemon rice hot.

BENGALI SPECIALITIES

Fish Curry with Mustard

PREP: *15 Mins* **COOK:** *30 Mins* **Servings:** *4*

4 fish steaks (500g)
2 tablespoons mustard seeds
1 tablespoon ginger
1 tablespoon garlic
2 green chilies
1 teaspoon turmeric powder
Salt to taste
2 tablespoons mustard oil
1 cup (250ml) water

1. Soak the mustard seeds in water, then grind them with the ginger, garlic, and green chilies into a paste.
2. Rub the fish with salt and half the turmeric powder. Heat the mustard oil and lightly fry the fish. Remove and keep aside.
3. Add the mustard paste, the rest of the turmeric powder, and salt to the same oil. Sauté for a few minutes.
4. Add water and bring to a boil. Add fish and simmer until the fish is cooked and the gravy thickens.
5. Serve the fish curry hot with rice.

Mishti Doi

PREP: *10 Mins* **COOK:** *2 Hour* **Servings:** *4*

4 cups (1L) milk
1 cup (200g) sugar
1 tablespoon plain yogurt

1. Boil the milk with the sugar until it reaches half its original volume.
2. Cool the milk until it is lukewarm. Add the yogurt and mix well.
3. Pour the milk into earthen pots and keep it warm for about 8-10 hours until it sets.
4. Refrigerate the mishti doi and serve chilled.

Sandesh

PREP: *15 Mins* **COOK:** *30 Mins* **Servings:** *4*

4 cups (1L) milk
Juice of 2 lemons
1/2 cup (100g) powdered sugar
1/2 teaspoon cardamom powder
A few strands of saffron

1. Boil the milk, then whisk in the lemon juice. Stir until the milk curdles. Strain to remove the whey and collect the chenna (curdled milk solids).
2. Knead the chenna with the sugar, cardamom powder, and saffron until smooth.
3. Shape the chenna into small discs or molds. Chill the sandwich before serving.

GUJRATI SPECIALITIES

Dhokla

PREP: *10 Mins* **COOK:** *20 Mins* **Servings:** *4*

1 cup (200g) gram flour (besan)
1 tablespoon semolina (sooji)
1 cup (240ml) buttermilk
1 teaspoon green chili ginger paste
Salt to taste
1 teaspoon fruit salt or Eno
2 tablespoons oil
1 teaspoon mustard seeds
1 teaspoon sesame seeds
Few curry leaves
Chopped cilantro (coriander) leaves for garnish

1. Mix the gram flour, semolina, buttermilk, chili-ginger paste, and salt into a smooth batter.
2. Add the fruit salt or Eno to the batter before steaming and mix well.
3. Steam the batter in a greased dish for 17-20 minutes until a tooth stick inserted comes out clean.
4. Heat the oil and add mustard seeds. When they crackle, add sesame seeds and curry leaves.
5. Pour this tempering over the steamed dhokla. Garnish with coriander leaves. Cut into pieces and serve.

Gujarati Kadhi

PREP: *10 Mins* **COOK:** *20 Mins* **Servings:** *4*

- 2 cups (500ml) buttermilk
- 2 tablespoons gram flour (be-san)
- 1 teaspoon ginger-green chili paste
- Salt to taste
- 1 tablespoon sugar
- 2 tablespoons oil
- 1 teaspoon mustard seeds
- 1 teaspoon cumin seeds
- Few curry leaves

1. Mix the buttermilk, gram flour, chili-ginger paste, salt, and sugar into a smooth mixture.
2. Simmer this mixture on low heat for about 15-20 minutes.
3. Heat the oil and add mustard seeds. Once they crackle, add cumin seeds and curry leaves.
4. Pour this tempering over the kadhi. Serve the Gujarati Kadhi hot with rice or roti.

Thepla

PREP: *15 Mins* **COOK:** *20 Mins* **Servings:** *4*

- 2 cups (250g) wheat flour
- 1 cup (100g) fenugreek leaves (methi), chopped
- 1 teaspoon ginger-green chili paste
- 1/2 teaspoon turmeric powder
- Salt to taste
- Oil for cooking

1. Mix the wheat flour, fenugreek leaves, chili-ginger paste, turmeric powder, and salt into a soft dough.
2. Divide the dough into small balls. Roll each ball into a thin disc.
3. Cook each thepla on a hot grill, using a little oil, until golden brown.
4. Serve the thepla hot with yogurt and pickle.

RAJASTHANI SPECIALITIES

Dal Baati Churma

PREP: *20 Mins* **COOK:** *1 Hour* **Servings:** *4*

Dal:
1 cup (200g) mix of lentils (moong, toor, chana)
Salt to taste
1 teaspoon turmeric powder
1 teaspoon chili powder
1 tablespoon oil
1 teaspoon cumin seeds
1 teaspoon garlic, finely chopped
1 teaspoon ginger, finely chopped
1 green chili, finely chopped
2 cups (500ml) water

Baati:
2 cups (250g) wheat flour
Salt to taste
½ cup (120ml) ghee

For the Churma:
1 cup (125g) wheat flour
½ cup (120ml) ghee
½ cup (100g) powdered sugar

1. Cook the lentils with salt, turmeric powder, chili powder, and water until soft.
2. Heat the oil and add cumin seeds. Add garlic, ginger, and green chili. Add the cooked lentils and simmer.
3. For the baati, mix the wheat flour, salt, and ghee into a stiff dough. Divide into balls and bake in an oven at 375°F (190°C) until golden brown.
4. For the churma, roast the wheat flour in ghee until golden brown. Cool and mix with powdered sugar.
5. Serve the dal with the baati and churma.

Gatte ki Sabzi

PREP: *15 Mins* **COOK:** *30 Mins* **Servings:** *4*

1 cup (200g) gram flour (besan)
Salt to taste
1 teaspoon chili powder
2 tablespoons oil
2 cups (500ml) water
1 teaspoon cumin seeds
½ teaspoon turmeric powder
1 cup (240ml) yogurt

1. Mix the gram flour, salt, chili powder, and oil into a stiff dough. Shape into thin cylinders and boil in water until cooked.
2. Cut the cooked gate into small pieces. Heat oil and add cumin seeds and turmeric powder. Add the yogurt and cook until it comes to a boil.
3. Add the gate and simmer until the gravy thickens. Serve the gatte ki sabzi hot with roti.

DESSERTS

Gulab Jamun

PREP: *20 Mins* **COOK:** *30 Mins* **Servings:** *6*

1¾ cups (200 grams) milk powder
2 tablespoons all-purpose flour
1/2 teaspoon baking soda
2 tablespoons ghee (clarified butter)
¼ cup (60 ml) milk
1 cup (200 grams) sugar
2 cups (500 ml) water
4 cardamom pods
2 cups (500 ml) vegetable oil for deep frying

1. Mix milk powder, all-purpose flour, baking soda, and ghee in a bowl. Add milk gradually to form a soft dough.
2. Divide the dough into small sections and shape each into a smooth ball.
3. Combine sugar, water, and cardamom pods in a deep pan to make the sugar syrup. Boil until the syrup is of one-string consistency.
4. In a separate pan, heat the oil. Deep fry every dough ball until golden brown.
5. Drain and immerse the fried balls in the sugar syrup. Leave them in the syrup for a few hours until they soak it up.
6. Serve the gulab jamuns warm or chilled.

Kheer

PREP: *10 Mins* **COOK:** *1 Hour* **Servings:** *4*

¼ (45 grams) Basmati rice
1-liter milk
¾ cup (150 grams) sugar
1/2 teaspoon cardamom powder
1 oz. (30 grams) raisins
1 oz. (30 grams) almonds, chopped

1. Wash the rice, then soak it for 30 minutes.
2. In a non-stick pan, add milk and take a boil.
3. Add the drained rice and add to the boiling milk.
4. Cook on low heat until the rice is soft and the milk is decreased to half.
5. Add sugar, cardamom powder, raisins, and almonds. Cook for another 5-10 minutes.
6. Serve the kheer hot or chilled.

Jalebi

PREP: *15 Mins* **COOK:** *30 Mins* **Servings:** *4*

7 oz. (200 grams) all-purpose flour
2 tablespoons yogurt
½ teaspoon baking powder
100 ml water
1 pinch saffron
1 cup (200 grams) sugar
2 cups (500 ml) oil for deep frying

1. Mix the all-purpose flour, yogurt, baking powder, and water to make a smooth batter. Leave it to ferment for 24 hours.
2. In a deep pan, prepare sugar syrup by boiling sugar and water until one-string consistency. Add saffron strands for color.
3. Heat oil in a frying pan. Pour the batter through a squeeze bottle or a cloth with a small hole into the hot oil in spirals. Fry until crisp.
4. Dip the fried jalebis in the hot (a little) sugar syrup for 2-3 minutes, ensuring they are thoroughly soaked.
5. Remove from the syrup and serve hot.

Laddoo

PREP: *10 Mins* **COOK:** *40 Mins* **Servings:** *4*

7 oz. (200 grams) gram flour (besan)
1 cup (200 grams) sugar
½ cup (120 ml) ghee (clarified butter)
¼ cup (50 grams) cashews, chopped
1/2 teaspoon cardamom powder

1. Heat 1/2 cup ghee (clarified butter) in a pan and add the gram flour. Roast on low heat until the golden brown flour releases a nutty aroma.
2. Remove the pan from the heat and let it cool slightly. Add sugar, cashews, and cardamom powder and mix well.
3. While the mixture is still warm, shape it into small, round laddoos. Allow them to cool completely before serving.

Carrot Halwa

PREP: *15 Mins* **COOK:** *45 Mins* **Servings:** *4*

1.1 lb. (500 grams) carrots, grated
1-liter milk
1 cup (200 grams) sugar
2 tablespoons ghee (clarified butter)
1/2 teaspoon cardamom powder
¼ cup (50 grams) almonds, chopped

1. In a heavy-bottomed pan, combine the grated carrots and milk. Cook on medium flame until the milk is fully absorbed.
2. Add sugar, ghee, cardamom powder, and chopped almonds, and cook on low heat until the mixture leaves the sides of the pan.
3. Serve the carrot halwa hot or chilled.

Rasmalai

PREP: *15 Mins* **COOK:** *45 Mins* **Servings:** *4*

1-liter milk
2 tablespoons lemon juice
1 cup (200 grams) sugar
1 teaspoon cardamom powder
¼ cup (50 grams) almonds and pistachios, chopped

1. Boil half of the milk and add lemon juice. Stir until the milk curdles completely. Strain the milk solids using a muslin cloth. Rinse under cold water to remove the sourness, then squeeze the excess water.
2. Knead the milk solids to make a smooth dough. Divide into small portions and flatten them into discs.
3. In a separate pan, boil the remaining milk with sugar until it reduces to half. Add cardamom powder.
4. Drop the milk discs into the reduced milk and cook for 10-15 minutes.
5. Chill the rasmalai before serving, and garnish with chopped nuts.

Barfi

PREP: *10 Mins* **COOK:** *20 Mins* **Servings:** *6*

2 cups (200 grams) grated coconut
1 cup (200 grams) sugar
¼ cup (60 ml) milk
1/2 teaspoon cardamom powder
2 tablespoons ghee (clarified butter)

1. In a pan, melt the ghee. Add the grated coconut and sauté for a few minutes.
2. Add sugar and milk and cook on a low flame until the mixture thickens and begins to leave the sides of the pan.
3. Add cardamom powder and mix well. Pour the mixture into the oil-greased tray and let it cool.
4. Cut into squares/diamond shapes and serve.

Sheera/Suji Halwa

PREP: *5 Mins* **COOK:** *20 Mins* **Servings:** *4*

4¼ oz. (120 grams) semolina
4¼ oz. (120 grams) sugar
2 cups (500 ml) water
¼ cup (60 ml) ghee (clarified butter)
1/2 teaspoon cardamom powder
¼ cup (50 grams) cashews and raisins

1. Heat 1/4 cup ghee (clarified butter) in a pan and roast the semolina until golden brown.
2. In a separate pan, boil the water and sugar until the sugar is completely dissolved.
3. Gradually add the sugar water to the roasted semolina, stirring continuously to avoid lumps.
4. Cook until the mixture thickens and leaves the pan's sides.
5. Add cardamom powder and garnish with cashews and raisins before serving.

Puran Poli

PREP: *20 Mins* **COOK:** *40 Mins* **Servings:** *6*

1 cup (200 grams) chana dal
1 cup (200 grams) sugar
1¾ cups (200 grams) wheat flour
¼ cup (60 ml) ghee (clarified butter)
1/2 teaspoon cardamom powder

1. Boil the chana dal until soft. Drain and grind to a fine paste. Mix with sugar and cardamom powder to make the filling.
2. Make a soft dough with flour and a little ghee.
3. Divide the dough into equal parts similarly for filling. Stuff each portion of the dough with the filling and roll it out into flatbreads.
4. Cook each poli on a hot grill, applying ghee on both sides. Serve hot.

Malpua

PREP: *10 Mins* **COOK:** *30 Mins* **Servings:** *4*

1 cup (120 grams) all-purpose flour
¼ cup (50 grams) semolina
1 cup (200 grams) sugar
2 cups (500 ml) milk
1/2 teaspoon cardamom powder
2 cups (500 ml) oil for deep frying

1. Make a batter with flour, semolina, sugar, and milk.
2. Heat oil in a pan. Drop a ladleful of batter into the oil and fry until golden brown.
3. Drain the malpuas and dip them in sugar syrup flavored with cardamom.
4. Drain from the syrup and serve hot.

Sandesh

PREP: *15 Mins* **COOK:** *30 Mins* **Servings:** *4*

1-liter milk
2 tablespoons lemon juice
3.5 oz. (100 grams) powdered sugar
1/2 teaspoon cardamom powder
2 oz. (55 grams) pistachios, chopped

1. Boil the milk, then drizzle and add the lemon juice. Stir until the milk curdles. Strain and rinse the milk solids under cold water to remove the sourness.
2. Squeeze out the excess water and knead the milk solids into a smooth dough.
3. Add powdered sugar and cardamom to the dough and knead until well combined.
4. Shape the dough into small discs and garnish with chopped pistachios.
5. Serve the sandesh at room temperature.

Shrikhand

PREP: *10 Mins* **COOK:** -- **Servings:** *4*

- 2 cups (500 grams) plain yogurt
- 3.5 oz. (100 grams) powdered sugar
- 1/2 teaspoon cardamom powder
- 2 oz. (55 grams) almonds and pistachios, chopped

1. Tie the yogurt in a cloth (muslin) and hag for a few hours to remove excess water.
2. Mix the thickened yogurt with powdered sugar and cardamom powder until well combined.
3. Chill the mixture in the refrigerator for a few hours.
4. Serve the shrikhand garnished with chopped nuts.

Phirni

PREP: *10 Mins* **COOK:** *30 Mins* **Servings:** *4*

2 oz. (55 grams) rice
1-liter milk
5.5 oz (150 grams) sugar
1/2 teaspoon cardamom powder
2 oz. (55 grams) almonds and pistachios, chopped

1. Soak the rice in water for a few hours, then grind it into a fine paste.
2. Boil the milk in a heavy-bottomed pan. Prepare rice paste and cook on a low flame, stirring continuously to prevent lumps.
3. When the mixture thickens, add sugar and cardamom powder. Cook for another few minutes.
4. Pour the mixture into serving dishes (individual) and chill in the refrigerator.
5. Serve the phirni garnished with chopped nuts.

Measurement Conversion Chart

Dry Measurements	
Measurement	**Equivalent**
1 Lb	16 ounces
1 cup	16 Tbsp
3/4 cup	12 Tbsp
2/3 cup	10 Tbsp plus 2 tsp
1/2 cup	8 Tbsp
3/8 cup	6 Tbsp
1/3 cup	5 Tbsp plus 1 tsp
1/4 cup	4 Tbsp
1/6 cup	2 Tbsp plus 2 tsp
1/8 cup	2 Tbsp
1/16 cup	1 Tbsp
1 Tbsp	3 tsp
1/8 tsp	Pinch
1/16 tsp	Dash
1/2 cup butter	1 stick of butter

Liquid Measurements	
Measurement	**Equivalent**
4 quarts	1 gallon
2 quarts	1/2 gallon
1 quart	1/4 gallon
2 pints	1 quart
4 cups	1 quart
2 cups	1/2 quart
2 cups	1 pint
1 cup	1/2 pint
1 cup	1/4 quart
1 cup	8 fluid ounces
3/4 cup	6 fluid ounces
2/3 cup	5.3 fluid ounces
1/2 cup	4 fluid ounces
1/3 cup	2.7 fluid ounces
1/4 cup	2 fluid ounces
1 Tbsp	0.5 fluid ounces

U.S. to Metric Conversions	
Measurement	**Metric Conversion**
Weight Measurements	
1 Lb	454 grams
8 ounces	227 grams
4 ounces	113 grams
1 ounce	28 grams
Volume Measurements	
4 quarts	3.8 liters
4 cups (1 quart)	0.95 liters
2 cups	473 milliliters
1 cup	237 milliliters
3/4 cup	177 milliliters
2/3 cup	158 milliliters
1/2 cup	118 milliliters
1/3 cup	79 milliliters
1/4 cup	59 milliliters
1/5 cup	47 milliliters
1 Tbsp	15 milliliters
1 tsp	5 milliliters
1/2 tsp	2.5 milliliters
1/5 tsp	1 milliliter
Fluid Measurements	
34 fluid ounces	1 liter
8 fluid ounces	237 milliliters
3.4 fluid ounces	100 milliliters
1 fluid ounce	30 milliliters

Oven Temperatures	
250°F	120°C
320°F	160°C
350°F	180°C
400°F	205°C
425°F	220°C

ISBN Paperback: 978-3-910634-25-1
ISBN Hardcover: 978-3-910634-26-8
Imprint: DJTS Publishing
info@djts-publishing.com

Made in the USA
Las Vegas, NV
08 October 2023